# Norwegian Forest Cats and Kittens

## The Complete Owners Guide

### Alex Halton

# Published by ROC Publishing 2014

## Copyright and Trademarks

## Disclaimer and Legal Notice

# Foreword

There are many reasons to be attracted to Norwegian Forest Cats. They are simply gorgeous, with their thick, plush coats and sweet, curious expressions. Although fully domesticated, there does seem to be something of the forest about these creatures with their tufted, Lynx-like ears.

If you consult the annals of Norwegian mythology the "Skogkatt" is certainly there, a magical creature of the woods, endowed with all sorts of powers.

I, personally, like to imagine these cats sailing with the Vikings, keeping their own counsel about what they witnessed and the new lands they visited.

Some accounts give this breed exotic blood brought to Europe by returning Crusaders, a fact the cat seems to confirm with those slightly oblique, vaguely Oriental eyes. But the thing I really like about Norwegian Forest Cats? They're big!

Some males reach a satisfying 16 lbs., putting them on par with the Maine Coon, another favorite of mine. I am an unabashed lover of big, purring couch potatoes.

And if you've never heard a Weegie purr, you are in for a treat! These beauties sound like well-tuned and powerful engines.

## Foreword

Perhaps the most important thing to know about the Norwegian Forest Cat, however, is its adaptability to all sorts of situations. I am an advocate for cats being kept indoors only. The Weegie does beautifully in a home.

He's a bit of a climber, but as long as you give him a good cat tree and lots of perches, he's well behaved, engaged, and delightfully connected to you and your family. He'll like the family dog, and Fido will, in spite of himself, return the regard.

Although long-haired, the Norwegian Forest Cat only sheds heavily in the spring, and doesn't require much in the way of grooming otherwise. They are hearty cats, but there are specific health conditions with the breed, which I will discuss in full in chapter four.

So long as you know these in advance and work with a reputable cattery, you will be able to find a healthy cat that should be with you for 14-16 years.

Weegies are excellent companions and among my favorite breeds. If you decide this is the right cat for you, you won't be disappointed.

Norwegian Forest cats are as endearing as they look, and justifiably one of the favorite breeds in both the United States and Canada with equal numbers of loyal adherants in Europe and around the world.

# Acknowledgments

## Thank you Poppy

# Acknowledgments

## Table of Contents

# Table of Contents

Table of Contents

# Table of Contents

## Chapter 1 – Meet the "Weegie"

It's just too much of a mouthful to say over and over again. "Yes. I have a Norwegian Forest Cat." These big, fluffy, playful, athletic beauties are known by the people who love them simply as Weegies.

While no cat is "just a cat," the Weegie is truly unique in the feline world. Its ancestors may well have handled rat control on Viking ships, and its blood lines are believed to connect with long-haired cats brought back to Europe by the Crusaders.

Certainly the Norwegian Forest Cat is a very old breed, one that almost went extinct before World War II, which would have been an incalculable loss in the world of cat fanciers.

In 1938, the first Norwegian Forest Cat Club was founded for the exclusive purpose of preserving the breed, although Weegies didn't actually leave Norway until the 1970s.

The breed was accepted for show status in Europe in 1977 and in the United States, Norwegian Forest Cats were granted championship status by the Cat Fanciers' Association in 1993.

Weegies are now extremely popular in Europe, America, and Canada, and are the official cat of Norway where they are known as the Skogkatt.

## Size and Shape

Weegies are big cats, averaging 14-16 lbs. They are slow to mature, rarely reaching full size until at least five years of age. They have a long lifespan of 14-16 years.

The breed is known for the striking beauty of its expression and facial features. Large, almond-shaped eyes are set obliquely in the face, which forms an equilateral triangle from the point of the nose to the base of the ears and across the forehead.

The profile is straight and clean from the ridge of the brow to the tip of the nose. The luxuriantly furnished ears compliment the long, flowing whiskers.

These cats are exceptional climbers thanks to their strong and sturdy claws. Don't think you can have a Weegie in the house without a tall, interesting cat tree. The breed is so adept at getting where they want to be, they can even clamber up rocks.

Pick a Weegie up and you'll be surprised by just how sturdy its body is under all that lovely fur. They are well muscled and big boned, with an oddly rugged overall appearance for a cat that looks out on the world with such a sweet and engaged expression.

## Coat and Colors

Like their close relative the Maine Coon, Weggies have semi-long coats. Although most often pictured as brown tabbies with white markings, all patterns and colors are acceptable except chocolate, lilac, fawn, and cinnamon.

The double coat evolved to withstand harsh winters. It serves as both superior insulation and waterproof protection from the elements. The softer undercoat is protected by a layer of coarse, long, guard hairs.

Even with this magnificent coat, complete with a full ruff, Weegies don't need the kind of constant brushing that characterizes the care regimen of other long-haired breeds.

Although Weegies are not any more difficult to care for than other breeds, they do go through heavy seasonal shedding in the spring. Then, there will be lots of cat hair on everything and everyone in the house.

That's when you'll want to bring out a soft brush and help your pet get rid of all that excess fur. (See the section on Daily Care for more information on grooming tools.)

## Disposition and Behavior

Both alert and intelligent, Weegies love to be with their humans, but prefer to keep things on their own terms. They are friendly and inquisitive with lots of energy to burn, and like most cats, they don't like to be ignored.

They are by turns both playful and cuddly, and will certainly be nearby and watching at all times. If you can't see your Weegie, look up. One of their favorite things to do is to find a high observation station and peer down at the world around them.

## With Dogs and Children?

Weegies are very good with children and unlike some breeds don't scurry away from activity. Whatever the family is doing, the cat will be right in the middle of it. They even react well to strangers.

Often termed a "dog lover's cat," the Norwegian Forest Cat gets on quite well with dogs, and in some instances will do much better with Fido than with another cat in the house. They have a fine disposition, but Weegies can be jealous if you're stepping out on them with another cat.

## With Other Types of Pets?

It's worth noting that Norwegian Forest Cats are highly adept hunters. If they are asked to live with animals that in their world view are prey, it takes a lot for Fluffy to restrain his natural urges.

This breed literally is descended from forest cats, and they are renowned as efficient mousers. To your cat, a hamster, gerbil, or guinea pig is just a higher class of mouse.

The same is true of their view towards fish and birds. Perhaps you've seen the cartoons at Christmas time where the cat asks, perplexed, "You put a tree full of shiny stuff in the middle of the living room and you don't want me to climb it?"

Think about presenting your cat with a bird in a cage, a fish in a bowl, or a "rat" in a box. In your cat's mind, you're giving him an edible present!

With a breed as talented at hunting as a Weegie, don't even think about keeping a companion rodent, fish, or bird unless everything is locked up hard and tight. You might even think about segregated living with the smaller, more vulnerable pets housed in a room of their own.

Many species of rodents can be literally frightened to death by nothing more than a cat sitting on top of their cage staring at them all day. Put yourself in your pet gerbil's place. That cat up there looks like exactly what it is, the Angel of Death with Fur!

## One Cat or Two?

Generally if you introduce a young Norwegian Forest Cat to a home with an existing cat, the animals will work everything out quite nicely on their own. It's somewhat harder to have a Weegie and then bring another cat into the mix since this is a disruption of your cat's cherished routine.

If you opt to adopt two cats from the same litter and raise them together, you will have an almost ideal situation. Litter mates who spend their entire lives together form a deep and special bond. They remain kittenish with one another throughout life and will be dedicated friends.

## Male or Female?

There really is little difference in disposition between the genders with Norwegian Forest Cats. They are very reliable and good-natured cats that adapt well to change and take most of life in stride.

The only major difference in the genders is that females tend to be slightly smaller. The primary concern people seem to have about adopting male cats is the wide misperception that all male cats are given to spraying pungent urine.

## My Opinion about "Spraying"

It is true that unaltered males of any breed might spray urine if they are around a female in heat, or if they feel a need to mark territory. This behavior is almost never seen in altered males unless they are seriously unhappy about something.

I have had exclusively male cats for 30 years, primarily because I like large cats, and I find that altered males of all breeds, including "alley cats" have lovely dispositions. In three decades of sharing my home with multiple "tomcats," as many as three and four at a time, I have never had a single instance of spraying.

Any time I am asked for advice by people who are experiencing spraying incidents with males, I invariably find a cat that is living with almost no positive interaction and enduring an absolutely filthy litter box. People do not understand just how fastidious cats are about their elimination habits.

In almost all of these cases, the people who own the cat, although perhaps quite well meaning, are casual cat owners who really have taken no time to understand the creatures with which they are sharing their homes.

Cats speak to us with a complex vocabulary of facial expressions, vocalizations, and body language. When a cat if exhibiting spraying behavior indoors, I look to what the humans are doing much more than to the cat. He's simply being a cat, and expressing his anxiety or unhappiness in a way that is natural to him.

The bottom line here is this. In my opinion, concerns about male cats spraying in the house are grossly inflated and mythologized. Happy, well-cared-for cats do not exhibit this behavior, and it should never be an issue with a breed as easygoing as a Norwegian Forest Cat.

## Indoors or Out?

Although Weegies are descended from superb hunters, these cats, like all domestic cats, should be kept indoors. It is not so much a matter of the cat's ability to adapt to the outdoors, as the fact that in the modern world "outdoors" is not safe for any beloved pet.

Whether the danger is from wild animals, neighboring dogs, or just vindictive humans, the danger is there, and it is real. Weegies live quite happily as exclusive indoor pets, enjoying plenty of perches near windows and interesting views.

Although they love to be with their humans, they are not needy cats. Your Weegie will learn your schedule quickly and adapt accordingly.

They are not given to the kind of separation anxiety seen in other breeds like the Siamese, which can yowl loud enough to wake the dead when it feels as if it's being neglected.

## Vocalizations

Weegies have quiet voices, with which they will greet you happily when you come home. In fact, this cat "talks" all the time, but it's a gentle running commentary heavily accented with an almost constant deep, throaty purr.

Certainly if they have to make noise, they can, and oddly enough if a Weegie is raised with a dog, it will be louder and more talkative — no doubt asserting its clear authority over the hapless canine. As a breed however, these cats are not given to "caterwauling."

## Norwegian Forest Cats and Allergies

The Norwegian Forest Cat is not one of the breeds considered to be either hypoallergenic or a low producer of Fel d 1, which is the primary feline allergen to which sensitive people react adversely.

Norwegian Forest Cats do not shed profusely year round, but they are a semi-longhaired breed. Fel d 1 is not just present in the dander from their fur, however, but also in the oil which naturally collects on surfaces the cat routinely touches.

# Chapter 1 – Meet the "Weegie"

# Chapter 2 – Locating and Working with a Breeder

In selecting a Norwegian Forest Cat breeder, you want to make sure that you are working with someone who has a well-established reputation of producing healthy, well-socialized animals.

The last thing you want to do is unwittingly support a backyard "breeder" who is basically running a "kitten mill." Stay away from ads in the classified section of the newspaper or signs tacked up on bulletin boards and street corners.

Operations that exist for no other purpose than ginning out litter after litter force their animals to live in overcrowded conditions. Often there's very little time out of the cage and almost no socialization. There may also be no concern about inbreeding, which raises the potential for all kinds of genetic defects.

It's fine to contact a breeder working from their home. That's actually a very standard arrangement for a cattery since such a facility is a 24/7 endeavor.

These are people who don't just raise cats though; they live with them. They add on rooms for their cats. They remodel the whole property. They live and breathe Norwegian Forest Cats.

When you work with a breeder of that quality, they are dedicated to preserving and enhancing the integrity of the breed. They're passionate and committed and will likely be interviewing you as much as you're interviewing them.

In order to contact breeders, you may want to attend local or regional cat shows. You won't be able to adopt a cat that day, but you will be able to get business cards from Norwegian Forest Cat exhibitors. Don't do more than that, however. At a show, a breeder really won't have time to talk to you, or let you handle the cats, so don't ask!

**What a Breeder Will Ask of You**

If you've never purchased a pedigreed cat from a breeder, you may have many misconceptions about the process. This is not going to be a matter of calling up a cattery, driving over, putting some money down, and walking out with a kitten. A breeder may well refuse to sell you a kitten if you don't meet their criteria for a good potential "parent."

Written agreements for the adoption of pedigreed cats generally include then following stipulations:

- The cat is to be spayed or neutered before 6 months of age.
- Within 72 hours of the adoption the cat will be evaluated by a vet.
- A written sales agreement must be signed.
- You will answer questions about your lifestyle and home.

Don't think, however, that breeders are heavy handed or unfriendly. They love their cats and they want to know their kittens are going to good homes.

It's perfectly normal after an adoption for the breeder to call you up just to see how things are going. They aren't being nosey. They care — and you want them to!

Staying on friendly terms with your breeder gives you ready access to an expert in the Norwegian Forest Cat breed. When you need advice or information, your breeder should be the first person you call.

**Be Sure to Ask the Breeder**

During the adoption interview, information will flow in both directions. The breeder should be open and receptive to answering questions. Getting any kind of "sales" talk should be a red flag. Most breeders will tell you far more about their catteries than you may want to know!

Remember that this whole process is about the long-term welfare of a living creature. The kitten is passing out of the breeder's care and into yours. Be sure that you get straightforward answers to questions like:

- Are the parent's healthy?
- Do you have their health records?
- Can I meet the parents?
- Has the kitten had any shots?
- Do you have those records?
- When are the booster shots due?
- Will I get copies of all the records?
- Has the kitten been evaluated for any specific disease?
- Has deworming been necessary?
- Has there been any other veterinary care?
- What are the specific guarantees that accompany the adoption?
- May I have references for former clients I can contact?

Reputable catteries are happy to answer these questions and many more.

Information should flow in both directions. Nothing offensive or intrusive is going on here. If a breeder asks you, "Where will the cat sleep?" or "What will you feed the cat?" answer! If you don't know, say so!

A breeder loves to hear a prospective parent say, "What would be the best thing to feed the kitten?" or "I'd like the cat to sleep with me. Do Norwegian Forest Cats like to do that?" (The answer is yes, by the way, and they're cover and pillow hogs.)

## Socialization Matters

Kittens born in catteries are generally not adopted before they are at least three months old. By then, they will be fully weaned from their mother's milk, litter box trained, and conversant with the use of a scratching post.

(You definitely want to ask about that last part. Weegies have strong claws and can be wicked about scratching if you don't give them the right thing to use.)

Socialization is also important. Kittens that transition well from a cattery to a new home have been:

- handled daily
- allowed free exploration time
- interacting with other cats
- playing with other kittens
- given lots of toys

- afforded a chance to climb / scratch on cat trees / posts
- engaged in active environments
- exposed to children and / or dogs
- introduced to a reasonable amount of noise

When kittens are raised without any experience with these factors, they may find moving to a new home harder. Although Weegies are not nervous cats by nature, it's always hard for a kitten to leave a known environment.

## How to Determine if a Kitten is Healthy

Although you should never ask to handle a kitten at a cat show, you'll want to spend time interacting with them at the cattery not only to make your choice, but to have a hands on evaluation of muscle tone and coat texture and quality.

Norwegian Forest Cat kittens should have clean, soft coats that show no signs of thinning. There should be no areas where the fur is missing. Gently blow on the fur to part it just a little so you can see the skin. There should be no flaking that indicates dry skin.

As you're playing with the baby, look at the area behind the ears, under the arms, and at the base of the tail on the underside. You don't want to find any flea "dirt," which is actually excreted blood. It will look like tiny, dark gravel.

Adopting a kitten with a flea or two is not unheard of, or cause for great alarm. Catteries wage a constant war on fleas. You do want to make sure the "passengers" are gone before you take the baby home, and you never want to see a profusion of fleas on a kitten.

Look into the kitten's eyes. Look for a return gaze that is bright, curious, interested and sweet. The eyes should not be crusted in the corners or show any evidence of discharge.

Make sure the baby isn't "snuffling" or sneezing. Upper respiratory infections can be problematic in catteries.

It's not unusual for any breed of kitten to be a little shy in the beginning, but within minutes the babies should be playing with you happily.

Ask for a toy or toys and see how the little ones react. Anticipate the pouncing response of miniature tigers!

There is no point, by the way, of dangling anything at a kitten that includes catnip unless the baby is 6-9 months old. Before that age, kittens exhibit no reaction to kitty "weed" whatsoever.

## Dealing with the Paperwork

When both you and the breeder are convinced that this is a good fit and the adoption moves forward, there's going to be a lot of paperwork. Be patient.

The basic purchase agreement will include the following items:

- clear indication of the breed being adopted
- description of color and pattern
- gender
- price
- names of the parents
- contact information for buyer and seller

Some of the specific provisions may include (but are not limited to):

- Agreement to provide veterinary care on a regular basis including the recommended course of vaccinations.

- Agreement to provide the necessary grooming required for the animal's coat as well as any other special grooming needs.

- Stipulation that there will be no refund if the cat is returned for any reason, and that if returned the animal must have been tested within the same week for ringworm, FELV/FIV, and fecal parasites.

It is standard practice for breeders to require clients to agree not to give away the kitten or to resell it without the breeder's written permission. Breeders do this not only to look out for the cat's welfare, but also to protect the genetic line they've worked hard to develop.

Breeders especially do not want to see their kittens given up to shelters, humane societies or pet stores. Breeders will take kittens back rather than see them put into such situations where, in all likelihood, they will be euthanized.

## Spaying and Neutering Required

Unless you have approached the breeder about a show animal you intend to breed, you must agree to spay or neuter the "pet quality" kitten you are adopting.

Essentially, the kitten is considered "flawed" in terms of its show quality, a fact that will be quite invisible to your eye.

Norwegian Forest Cat

Breeders ask that these kittens be spayed or neutered as a further measure to protect their carefully cultivated bloodlines.

Generally the surgery must be performed before the cat reaches six months of age and you will need to provide proof in the form of a veterinary receipt. (Typically you won't receive the cat's full papers until this stipulation has been met.)

**Declawing is Forbidden**

The paperwork will also require you to agree never to have the kitten declawed. This practice is actually illegal in Europe, and also in some parts of the United States as an inhumane act.

The last digit of the cat's toe must be amputated to remove the claw, which is not only painful, but will affect the animal's future mobility and will deprive the cat of its primary means of self-defense.

With proper training, regular claw clipping, and the availability of scratching posts and trees, there will be no need for such an unnecessary and radical measure.

**Known Genetic and Health Issues**

In the chapter on health, I will discuss some of the medical issues that can be present in Norwegian Forest Cats. Your adoption papers should include a health guarantee and an indication of whether or not the kitten and its parents have been evaluated for any of these problems.

The required veterinary checkup within 72 hours is intended as a verification of this guarantee. You will also be asked to supply a receipt to prove that this check has been performed.

**Things to Know Before You Bring Kitty Home**

When you transition a kitten out of the cattery and into your home, try to keep everything "the same," especially in terms of food and litter box arrangements.

Ask the breeder what kind of food the kitten has been eating, and what kind of litter and box has been used. Cats are particular creatures. They care about texture. One cat likes chunky food and gravel litter; another insists on paté and sand. This is important information to ask the breeder if you don't want kitty to go "off" either habit, honor these preferences.

Any changes should be introduced slowly and with the understanding that you may very likely lose the battle. Some cats are quite set in their ways from an early age.

Buy kitten safe toys. Pay special attention to anything that might create a hazard of choking. Some toys should only be used with you there to supervise. These include items with strings, feathers, bells, and similar attachments.

Make sure all the other supplies you will need are in place, including grooming implements. Norwegian Forest Cats don't need to be brushed more than once a week since they only shed heavily in the spring, but they do like the attention!

Get them used to being brushed as kittens and you won't have any problems when you do need to help your cat get rid of loose fur.

## Cat Proof the House

Never underestimate a kitten's ability to get into trouble, especially with a breed that likes to climb as much as Weegies do.

Kittens are unbelievably curious. They have no understanding of just how little they are, and they'll try just about anything. (Not to mention the fact that they don't always learn from their mistakes.)

Get anything out of the area that your baby might get tangled in or swallow. Be especially careful about electrical cords.

Even if the kitten doesn't chew on the cable, they might pull something down. Tape wires to the baseboards and cap open electrical outlets.

Use baby latches on cabinet doors, in particular those where household chemicals are stored.

## Bringing the Kitten Home

Ask the breeder for any other advice about bringing your kitten home, especially if there are other pets in the house. On a whole, Norwegian Forest cats are highly adaptable.

Still, it's a good idea to let kittens get used to things in a segregated area for the first few days. If there are other pets, this allows for a lot of sniffing through the safety of closed doors and tentative initial paw contact.

Handle the first face-to-fact introduction carefully with no overreactions. The last thing you want is for your pets to pick up on your tension. Let the animals work it out, but be ready to go to the rescue if necessary.

Generally within 7-10 days, kittens are well established and in their minds running the show. All territorial issues should be resolved within that period and the "pecking order" sorted out.

## Approximate Costs

For a "pet" quality Norwegian Forest Cat kitten, expect to pay $885 (£550) to $1375 (£853).

In terms of, monthly and annual costs, a Norwegian Forest Cat is no more expensive than any semi long-haired breed.

For a pet-quality Norwegian Forest Cat, and assuming a lifespan of 14-16 years, the cost of keeping the cat will be $21,910 to $25,040 / £13,595 to £15,537.

That breaks down to $1,565 / £1,028 a year, or $130 / £85.40 a month.

(Note that with show cats that are being actively exhibited, other expenses will come into play like professional grooming, entry fees, travel, memberships, registrations, and so on.)

# Chapter 3 – Daily Care Needs

One of the greatest misconceptions that I would like to dispel about all cats, not just Norwegian Forest Cats, is the notion that felines are aloof creatures that do not require interaction from their humans.

## Breaking Stereotypical Expectations

Certainly some cat breeds have general reputations for being either aloof or social. Disposition, however, is actually more a factor of individual personality than breed. Many cats pick out one person on whom they lavish their

---

attention and loyalty in private while ignoring or outright avoiding everyone else.

The important point is that the stereotype of all cats as self-sufficient loners is simply not true. I have been a cat owner all my life and in that time, I have only met one cat with whom I could not make friends.

She was a Somali, a breed the American Cat Fancier's Association calls "the epitome of everything most people want in a companion animal." The one I knew hated everyone and was, frankly, rather possessed. Breed is not always an indicator of personality!

## Your Pet's Emotional Needs

It should go without saying that you are responsible for meeting your cat's physical needs. You have an additional responsibility, however, to make sure that your pet gets the emotional engagement it requires to be happy and well-adjusted. This is particularly important with Norwegian Forest Cats, due to their strong trait of companionability with their people.

## Speaking "Cat"

Typically, Weegies are not given to "getting into trouble." Any cat, however, that is bored, or feeling ignored, can certainly make its opinions known -- generally in a way that you're not going to like.

Beyond the obvious pleasure that you will take in interacting with your pet, being completely engaged in your cat's life also enables you to observe the animal, and to head off any health conditions or behavioral issues before they become serious.

Understanding your pet will stem from the simple fact that you will, over time, learn to speak "cat." If you have never had a cat before, you may not realize that you are developing a relationship with a highly intelligent animal. This meeting of minds must surmount not just a language barrier, but also a species barrier.

Your cat will think like a cat, and communicate his thoughts accordingly. You think like a human, which the cat probably sees as your major failing in life!

Here's a good example. Many people believe that they can effectively get a cat's attention by yelling at the animal. Feline hearing is geared much more towards subtle and high-pitched sounds.

If it looks like your cat is ignoring you when you yell, he is. Try whispering instead. You will likely be shocked at the reaction. Fluffy's ears will go up, rotate in place, and zero in on the sound of your voice.

This is precisely the same behavior the cat would exhibit if he were locating a tiny mouse rustling behind the sofa clear across the room.

Since the cat will pretty much refuse to learn your language, it behooves you to learn his! Trust me on this fact; it will make your life a lot easier, and lower the frustration level for your cat who is saddled with dealing with a "stupid human."

## Feeding Your Cat

One sound that will awaken any sleeping cat regardless of how far away he is in the house from the kitchen is the sound of a pull tab on a can of cat food.

It is also a stereotype that all cats are finicky, but they do have definite likes and dislikes when it comes to what goes in their food bowl.

### Emphasize High-Quality Nutrition

While it may be more convenient for you to simply leave out a bowl of dry food for your cat, these animals are carnivores. They need protein, which means a well-balanced diet of both dry and wet food.

### *Wet vs. Dry Food*

Many owners believe that if they feed their cats wet food they will have more mess to clean up in the litter box. If you are dealing with a lot of litter box odor, and copious amounts of solid waste, you're feeding your cat something that doesn't agree with his digestive system.

Instead of eliminating wet food, which is also a critical source of moisture, you need to experiment and find a canned food that your pet tolerates more efficiently.

An additional argument for feeding a diet of both dry and wet food is the matter of weight control. Cats that eat exclusively dry food tend to weigh more. Those that eat wet food, as part of a well-balanced combination diet, maintain a healthier body weight.

### Food Selection and Body Weight

One of the best ways to determine if your cat is maintaining a good weight is simply to look at the animal from above. If you can see a slight indentation behind the rib cage and before the hips begin, your cat's figure is looking good!

It is never smart to get your cat started on human food. There is no reason to believe that your cat has any more self-control than you do!

Once Fluffy has developed a sweet tooth, he will become a highly talented panhandler, pulling out all of the stops to convince you that he is completely starving to death.

If you fall for this, you will, in short order, have an overweight cat that is susceptible to all of the diseases and body conditions that go with weight gain. These may be as serious as diabetes, and as debilitating as joint disease.

### Toxic Foods

There are some items that you should never give your cat due to the high danger of toxicity. These include, but are not limited to alcoholic beverages, avocados, raisins, grapes, eggs, garlic, onions, and chives. Never give your cat any sort of yeast dough.

Caffeine in any form can be deadly to cats, and under no circumstances should they ever be allowed access to chocolate, which contains methylxanthines found in cacao seeds.

The same extract that is used in chocolate is also present in a variety of other beverages including soda. If your cat is exposed to these items, the range of symptoms can be serious and life-threatening, including excessive thirst, panting, vomiting, diarrhea, irregular heartbeat, seizures, and tremors.

It's also important to make sure that your cat never has access to anything that includes xylitol, which is a sweetener. Exposure to this chemical can result in liver failure. Also, do not let your animal have salty treats.

Dehydration is a significant health risk in cats. They should never go without water for any length of time or be exposed to items that creates excessive thirst.

### The Milk Myth

It comes as a serious shock to most people that the notion that milk or cream is good for cats is really something of a myth. This is not to say that if offered these items Fluffy will not take them, and enjoy them. But again, do not assume that cats always know what's good for them!

The real story on the matter of milk is that cats do not produce enough of the enzyme lactase to allow milk to be broken down in their digestive systems. The result is generally a case of diarrhea and certainly gastrointestinal upset that is extremely uncomfortable.

This is not at all unlike lactose intolerance in humans. If you have this problem, or if you know anyone who does, you certainly do not want to subject your beloved pet to that level of physical distress!

The truth is that an adult cat does not require milk, and they are not going to get any real nutritional benefit from it for the simple reason that they are not cows. Every species of mammal produces milk that is appropriate for its young and its young only.

There is nothing wrong with giving your cat the occasional dish of milk as a treat, but do not make it a regular occurrence. If there is any sign of stomach upset, immediately stop offering the milk.

*Free Feeding*

There are some cat breeds with which you simply cannot follow a practice of free feeding, which means leaving dry food in their bowl at all times. The Russian Blue, for instance, is extremely given to weight gain, and will show no restraint whatsoever if food is left out.

Typically this is not a problem with a Norwegian Forest Cat, however, you do need to observe your pet's food intake. If you begin to see that Fluffy is putting on a few pounds, instigate a program of regular feedings.

Also remember that as a breed, Norwegian Forest Cats mature slowly. Your cat will not reach its full size until at least five years of age, and for that period of time may require more food. After age five, monitor your pet's meals more closely, and perhaps cut back on the amount of food offered.

## Picking Dry and Wet Foods

Again, cats are carnivores, and they cannot be made vegetarians. For this reason, when you read the list of ingredients on the label of a food that you are considering, the first item should be meat. As a general rule of thumb, the less expensive the food, the more grain it will contain as filler.

Discuss the matter of food with the breeder from whom you acquired your Norwegian Forest Cat. Certainly in the beginning, you should give the kitten whatever it has been accustomed to receiving to avoid any gastrointestinal upset.

It is likely that you should follow the breeder's recommendation for food in the future as well, so long as you can afford the items recommended. Everyone is subject to unique budgetary concerns, but using a high-quality food is a critical component of preventive health care for your pet.

**Considering the Raw Diet**

In recent years the raw diet has been advocated for both dogs and cats, but this feeding program remains controversial. I mention it here not to advocate using or avoiding the method, but only to give you some basic information about this nutritional approach.

The theory is a simple one; giving your pets the raw food they would consume were they living in the wild and hunting on their own. As carnivores, this means for cats the equivalent of fresh, whole animal carcasses including bones.

This last fact alone is sufficient to give most veterinarians and many confirmed cat lovers reason to reject the raw concept. Even well-ground bones can raise a choking hazard. Swallowing bone shards create a serious danger of throat, stomach, and intestinal lacerations.

There is also a risk of salmonella poisoning, which is only partially mitigated by the presence of strong bacteria in the cat's stomach. When the raw diet is handled appropriately, it requires meticulous preparation with special equipment in absolutely sanitary conditions.

The diet relies on raw chicken and beef only, with no pork included. Even when refrigerated, the food must be used in 2-3 days or discarded, and it must never be microwaved.

This is a method of feeding your pet that requires careful research and full consultation with your veterinarian. There is a great deal more involved to managing complete nutrition for your cat in this way than simply putting some raw meat in his bowl.

---

*Estimating Food Costs*

This is, frankly, next to impossible. There are simply too many brands and too many options. Keep your attention focused on the quality of the nutrition and buy the best food you can possibly afford.

As a conservative estimate based on my own experience, you will spend about $50/£33 per month per cat on wet food and about $25/£17 on dry.

*Frequency of Feeding*

It's alright to experiment with free feeding your cats dry food. Try to limit the daily serving to about .25-.50 US cups (0.108-0.416 UK cups.)

Put out wet food twice a day, Each serving should be approximately 5.5 ounces / 14.17 grams.

**Considering Food Bowls**

Norwegian Forest Cats have absolutely gorgeous long, flowing whiskers. As a result, they may be prone to "whisker stress."

Essentially, when the cat puts its face in a normal bowl, the sensation of its whiskers rubbing against the sides is uncomfortable for the animal.

You can always tell when a cat is experiencing whisker stress because they'll reach into the bowl, grab a big bite, and then drop it on the floor right beside the bowl.

For cats that exhibit this problem, choose a feeding dish that is a shallow tray. Regular food and water bowls cost about $5-$10 / £3-£7.

Expect to pay about $25/£16 for a whisker stress-free bowl. (These trays are typically on legs for stability and slight elevation.)

**The Importance of Water**

Cats are particular about their water bowls, and will not drink from a dirty container or one in which the water has been allowed to become stale.

It is extremely important that your cat have a constant supply of clean, fresh water that is changed on a daily basis.

Norwegian Forest Cats are not one of the breeds that have a reputed fondness for playing in water, but all cats are more likely to drink from a running water source than from a bowl. For this reason, I'm a big advocate of feline water fountains.

These units are no longer expensive, selling for about $30/£23.

## The All-Important Litter Box

The number one cited reason for companion cats being given up to shelters is litter box issues. I have to be honest. This makes my blood boil.

Cats are fastidious creatures. When they go "off" their litter box, they are either physically ill or they have a lousy cleaning staff -- you!

I always ask owners the same question, "Would you use it?" Cats have 200 million odor-sensitive receptors in their

noses. You have 5 million. If you think the box smells bad, imagine what you're asking Fluffy to climb into!

When a cat starts to exhibit unusual litter box habits, immediately have your pet evaluated for kidney or bladder conditions.

If your pet is going to his box and experiencing pain there, he'll start looking for someplace to go where it doesn't hurt. In his mind, the pain and the location are associated.

If there is no health problem, evaluate the state of the box. If you're scooping daily and keeping odors in check, move on to the kind of box you're giving your cat and the texture of the litter.

Many cats do not like open litter pans. For them, it's the equivalent of leaving the bathroom door open. They don't want to be watched! Others absolutely hate the feel of gravel on their paws, preferring nice, smooth sand.

In the beginning, use whatever your kitten has been accustomed to at the breeder's. Typically cats get used to one type of litter and litter box arrangement and prefer to use it for life. (In case you don't know it, cats aren't big on change.)

If you do want to use a different type of box or an alternate litter, never take away the old box until Fluffy is reliably using the new box or disaster may ensue!

Cats live in a world of smells. Once Fluffy has urinated or defecated in an area, to his nose, that is an acceptable place to "go."

Always clean up any accidents with special enzymatic cleaners that remove all traces of the offending by-product. Nature's Miracle makes an excellent line of cleaners that sell for $5-$10/£3-£6.

## Available Litter Types

Your choices in litter types are no longer limited to the traditional gravel, but that's a good starting point to consider both texture and expense.

### Gravel or Clay

This is your most economical choice, with 10 lbs. (4.53 kg) selling for as little as $2.50-$5.00 (£2-£4).

### Fine Clumping Sand

Clumping sand is very popular, especially because some formulas are designed specifically for multiple cat households. The biggest drawback to sand is how easily it flies all over the place.

The most important thing to remember? Don't flush this stuff unless the box specifically says you can!

Clumping litters are more expensive. Mainstream brands purchased in bulk average $18 / £12 for 42 lbs. (19 kg).

So called "designer" brands that reputedly do a better job controlling odors are much more costly, with just 1.4 lbs. (.63 kg) retailing for $30 / £20

## *Environmentally Friendly Litters*

These products are plant-based and are typically made of material like pine, which is a cost effective solution if your cat will use them.

These litters tend to be very lightweight, and many cats don't seem to think they "feel" like something they'd use to do their "business."

Pine litter sells for approximately $10 / £7 for 20 lbs. (9.07 kg).

## *Crystals*

Absorbent crystals are the latest innovation in cat litter. They are intended to inhibit bacterial growth by absorbing and trapping urine in biodegradable amorphous silica gel. You will pay, on average, $16 / £11 for 8 lbs.

Cats do have definite preferences for litter texture. If you are going to attempt to transition your cat to a new type of litter, offer him two boxes: one with the new litter, and one with what he's used to OR mix the two litter types, gradually phasing out the old litter.

If you just present your cat with a box full of something completely new, don't be surprised if you get a . . . surprise.

## Litter Box Types

Although sizes and shapes vary, you will have a choice of three types of litter box:

- open pan
- covered box
- self-scooping

The open pan is the old standard, and the most economical at $6-$10 / £4-£6. This arrangement does lead to a lot of scattering and many cats just do not like to be watched. You can get around this preference by locating the pan in an out-of-the-way place and/or put a screen around it.

Covered boxes give cats a sense of privacy, and they are much less unsightly in your environment. Many have filters in the lid to help control both dust and odor. Depending on size and configuration, budget $30-$50 / £20-£33.

Humans like the automatic self-scooping boxes, but some cats will flee in terror (or try to attack and dismantle the "monster" on sight.)

If you can get your cat to use one of these boxes, your days of scooping are pretty much over, although the pan will need to be washed out from time to time.

You will spend approximately $150 to $200 (£98-£130) for an automated litter box, but a word to the wise — don't get rid of the old box until you're sure Fluffy is on board with technological innovation!

## Exercise, Play, and Training

The words "train" and "cat" were once considered to be mutually exclusive. That was before cat shows began to include feline agility competitions. It is important to understand from the beginning, however, that even though your cat loves you, he's not a dog.

Seems like an obvious statement? Here's the real difference. Dogs have an innate desire to please. They are pack animals. You are the alpha. Dogs perform tricks to make you happy.

Cats are solitary hunters. They have to be shown a reason to "perform." This may well be getting to interact with you, but that's not where you'll be in the beginning.

When you first try to get desired responses out of your Norwegian Forest Cat, you should cater to whatever your pet does naturally.

If, for instance, you have a cat that likes to use his paws, you can work for tricks that involve a paw touch, then build on that behavior with more complex sequences.

The important thing is always to reward positive responses, and just ignore the rest. There should be no negative reinforcement, no scolding, no expressions of frustration, and certainly no yelling. Keep any training session under 15 minutes, and always pair rewards with verbal affirmations.

Over the years I've had cats that would give me "high fives," leap to my shoulder when I patted it, and retrieve specific toys by name.

On average cats can learn 35-50 words, although I have had pets that knew far more — and some that knew far less. I recommend just playing with your cat and letting any "tricks" evolve naturally.

The more opportunities you provide your Norwegian Forest Cat to indulge his natural proclivities, the more chances you'll have to turn normal behaviors into "tricks."

For instance, Weegies are premier climbers. Invest in the most elaborate cat tree you can fit in your house. Get something interesting with perches and tunnels. This is not just a play and exercise area, but important protection for your home.

A simple little $30/£20 scratching pole is not enough for a Weegie!  Expect to invest anywhere from $100 (£65) to $300 (£197) and up to get a cat tree they'll really love and on which they'll take out their natural urge to scratch.

If that's not enough to keep your cat from attacking the furniture you have a number of options for deterrents. My favorites are herbal preparations and adhesive strips.

Cats don't like either pennyroyal or orange essence. Spray bottles of these mixtures sell for $12-$15 / £7.87-£9.84.

---

Fluffy will also dislike anything "tacky" under his paws. Double-sided adhesive strips are an excellent and affordable way to discourage scratching. They're priced at about $8-$10 / £5.25-$6.56 per package.

## Grooming Needs

Even with their heavy double coats, a Norwegian Forest Cat is very easy to groom. A brushing once a week will suffice to keep the stray hair down until spring, which is the major shedding season. Then, you may find that you're brushing daily for a couple of weeks.

Combing and brushing is very good for both your cat's skin and coat, however, just make certain you don't pull at the coat. For a Weegie, you'll want a brush with widely spaced individual bristles on a bed of rubber.

These are typically called "pin cushion" brushes. They sell for $7-$10 (£5-£7). Also keep a wide, wire-toothed comb on hand. They cost $10-$12 (£7-£8).

Thankfully the cost of a Norwegian Forest Cat seldom mats or tangles. If, however, your cat's coat does develop mats, don't try to cut them out. You could seriously harm your pet's fragile skin. Get the help of a professional groomer who has the correct tools.

# Chapter 4 – Health Care Facts

Cats are not unlike humans when it comes to the potential of inheriting a physical problem or a disease. Norwegian Forest Cats are typically long lived and healthy cats, especially when they are cared for by attentive and observant human companions.

## Potential Genetic Illnesses

There are, however, three conditions that can occur in Weegies, of which you should be aware: hypertrophic cardiomyopathy, hip dysplasia, and glycogen storage disease type IV.

### Potential for Hypertrophic Cardiomyopathy

Hypertrophic cardiomyopathy or HCM is a genetic disorder that causes the heart muscle to thicken. It is the most common cardiac disease present in all cat breeds, and can be confirmed with an echocardiogram.

Eventually, cats affected with HCM will suffer from accumulation of fluid in the lungs and blood clots before dying of heart failure. There is no cure for this condition.

Do not believe any breeder that makes a claim that his line is HCM free. There is no way to guarantee that any cat won't develop the problem.

Most breeders are quite prepared to discuss this fact openly, and to disclose to what extent HCM has been present in their animals.

### Hip Dysplasia

Hip dysplasia is caused by a defect in the hip socket that may cause your cat to move slowly or to be reluctant to climb and jump. The degree to which mobility is affected may be mild and painless, or debilitating.

Helping the cat to maintain a normal body weight is a critical component in managing hip dysplasia. Medication may be necessary for pain, and surgery is also an option.

## Glycogen Storage Disease Type IV

Cats suffering from glycogen storage disease type IV are deficient in the enzyme needed to metabolize glycogen. Typically, kittens with this condition die in the womb. Cats that survive experience fever, weakness, and muscle tremors.

In some rare cases it is possible to regulate hypoglycemia in cats with high-carbohydrate diets and frequent portions, but there is no cure for this disease.

All types of glycogen storage disease or glycogenosis are fatal in the vast majority of cases, and often euthanasia is necessary because the physical deterioration is progressive and severe.

## Routine Health Care

The primary foundation of routine health care for your cat is finding a veterinarian you trust who has extensive experience with purebred cats. Although it is certainly possible for any small animal veterinarian to treat your cat, you may opt for a feline-specific practice.

Vet clinics devoted exclusively to the care of cats have become popular in the last 10 years and can offer significant advantages.

The offices are quieter, and tend to be easier for skittish and nervous cats because there are no barking dogs or disturbing odors that fall outside the cat's perception of the "normal" world. Fluffy may not like smelling another cat in his near environment, but he'll like smelling a strange dog less.

Additionally, veterinarians at cat-only practices stay on the cutting edge of developments in feline medicine. Since most pet owners prefer to keep one vet for the course of their animal's life, make this choice carefully.

You may want to make an appointment with the vet specifically to discuss becoming a client, leaving Fluffy at home.

Make it clear when you book the time that you are coming to meet the vet and see the clinic, but will be paying for a regular office visit.

Have your questions prepared in advance and don't overstay. Vets are busy medical professionals. If you like the clinic, the staff, and the doctor, make a second appointment to go in with your cat.

As a new cat owner, the first health care matters that will require attention are spaying / neutering and vaccinations.

**Spaying and Neutering**

The Norwegian Forest Cat you've adopted will likely be a "pet quality"animal. This simply means that for some reason, your pet doesn't conform to the accepted breed standard to be shown. You probably won't be able to see the "problem" even when it's pointed out to you, so don't worry about it.

The reason you are required to spay or neuter your pet, however, is not only to cut down on the shocking number of unwanted animals in the world, but also to protect the breed itself.

Catteries are constantly working to improve the blood lines they cultivate, and they do not want to see perceived flaws passed on.

This is a condition of the adoption, requiring your agreement to produce proof of the surgery before six months of age. Since this is the optimal period of time for either surgery to be performed, this is a very routine and low risk matter.

Price varies by clinic. Certainly there are low cost options as affordable as $50 (£32.82).

However, since being either spayed or neutered is the first medical procedure your cat will require, this is an excellent time to have the surgery performed by the vet of your choice and to get your cat's medical records in place at the practice. For this reason, cost may not be the primary factor in determining where your cat will be "fixed."

**Routine Vaccinations**

Although vaccinating pets against contagious disease has been an important component of health care for companion animals for decades, the topic remains controversial. A primary concern is the potential for the development of injection site tumors.

If you are uncertain about vaccinating your cat, discuss the topic fully with your breeder and veterinarian and conduct research on your own.

By the time you welcome your Weegie into your home, it will already have received its primary shots. It will be your decision about continuing with the "boosters."

# Chapter 4 – Health Care Facts

The recommended program of vaccinations for cats includes the following:

## Distemper Combo

The distemper combo shot is given at 6 weeks of age, with repeat "boosters" administered every 3-4 weeks until the kitten is 16 weeks old. A second booster is given at one year, then every three years for life.

The injections are intended to provide protection against:

- panleukopenia (FPV or feline infectious enteritis)

- rhinotracheitis (FVR, an upper respiratory / pulmonary infection)

- calicivirus (causes respiratory infections)

Some forms of the vaccine include protection against Chlamydophilia, which causes conjunctivitis.

## Feline Leukemia

The feline leukemia vaccination is given at age 2 months with a booster indicated 3-4 weeks later. Beginning at one year of age, the cat will receive annual boosters for life.

Feline leukemia is a highly infectious disease that can be transmitted from one cat to another by little more than a "nose tap."

If there is any chance of your pet coming into contact with other cats, especially those that live outside, this is an important vaccination.

## *Rabies*

Generally local law mandates the administration of rabies vaccinations on an annual basis with proof of compliance maintained by the pet owner. Rabies vaccinations cost approximately $40 (£26) per injection.

## Practicing Preventative Healthcare

Cats deal with pain much differently than we do. In their world view, showing pain or physical distress opens them up to attack from larger animals. Rather than appear vulnerable, a cat will hide its discomfort until the illness becomes very serious.

As a vigilant and loving pet owner, you will know your Norwegian Forest Cat better than anyone. In handling your pet each day, you can be aware of indicators of potential problems, as well as be sensitive to subtle changes in mood and behavior.

Do not be concerned about being perceived as a worried and obsessed "parent." Go with your gut. If you think something is wrong with your cat, there probably is something wrong. Call the vet!

Some signs to watch for on a routine basis include:

- Weight loss or gain. Healthy cats have a fat pad over their ribs, but you should still be able to feel the bones.

- Changes in gait, or a reluctance to run or jump. These problems can indicate issues with muscle damage, joint pain, or even the presence of a growth that is hindering motion.

- A dry or runny nose. A normal cat's nose is clean and moist, not cracked and dry or running with clear or discolored mucus.

- Discharge from the eyes. Norwegian Forest Cats have bright, interested eyes with a sweet and engaged expression. Make sure the pupils are centered and that the white of the eye shows only minimal blood vessels and no discoloration.

- Ear tenderness or significant debris. Cats are prone to ear parasites, infections, and other irritations. Make sure there is no foul odor in your cat's ear. If you see a lot of debris rather than a smooth, clean surface, and if there is redness present, the vet needs to take a look.

- Pale gums or yellowed teeth. Your cat's gums should be pink and healthy, and the teeth should be white and free of yellowing or dark build-up indicating plaque. Regular dental exams are also important to detect any lumps or lesions since all cats are prone to oral cancers. If detected early, such growths can be managed with some degree of success.

Dental care is so important that if your cat is willing, it's a good idea to brush Fluffy's teeth. Yes, it sounds nuts, but vets carry oral hygiene kits and are happy to help you learn how to successfully perform regular dental care at home.

This does not replace annual cleanings, but can still significantly improve the overall condition of your cat's mouth. The kits cost about $7-$10 (£4.60-£6.56) each.

Also be aware of the following:

- Respiration. Your cat should breathe from the chest, not the abdomen.

- Growths, bumps, or masses. Anything of this sort should be evaluated by your vet.

- Litter box behavior. When a cat "misses" or goes outside the box, the animal may be suffering from an undiagnosed or chronic kidney or bladder infection.

Norwegian Forest Cats are typically healthy cats with a zest for life. They are active and social without being intrusive. This fact alone is an important part of your preventive health care "plan."

If you detect a change in your cat's behavior, try to find out why immediately. Don't wait, or you may allow a minor problem to become more serious.

# Chapter 4 – Health Care Facts

# Chapter 5 – Breeding and Showing

Breeding cats is one of those things that sounds like a good idea the first time you say it; then the careful consideration needs to kick in. This is not some idle hobby, nor is it a way to make a lot of money, which often surprises people or causes them to scoff in disbelief.

It's true that Norwegian Forest Cat kittens and those of other pedigreed breeds sell for high prices. Behind those high prices, however, are a long line of bills at the cattery just waiting to be paid.

Professional breeders get into the business for one reason — love of the breed. Most will tell you they're just happy if they break even.

## Considering Becoming a Breeder

My best advice for people considering becoming cat breeders is to immerse themselves in the culture of cat shows, and in particular of the breed in which you're interested.

Go to events to meet existing Norwegian Forest Cat breeders, or simply to get their business cards and make contact later. (As you will soon come to understand, cat shows are hectic and you don't want to get in the way or be a pest.)

Online discussion forums are also an excellent resource, but don't just dive in. Forum etiquette can be tricky. "Lurk" for a few weeks and learn how people interact on the venue. It's far easier to give offense in such a setting than you may realize.

### Critical Questions

Not only are you attempting to learn more about breeding in general and Norwegian Forest Cats in particular, you're trying to arrive at answer to crucial questions that only you can address — and I don't mean knee jerk answers. These are matters you must consider carefully and seriously.

*Is this a commitment I can really make?*

Actually, there are multiple commitments to consider: time, money, and space. You'll give up a lot of nights, weekends, and holidays. Your schedule will be dominated by the needs of the animals that depend on you completely.

Have you thought about that responsibility? Are you prepared for the losses? For the kittens that don't make it? Or for the day when you have to give those kittens up to their new homes?

No matter how carefully you screen every adoption, you're still going to have to send your "babies" home with someone else.

*Do you have a plan for the logistics of getting set up?*

Not only do you have to finance getting a breeding pair of Norwegian Forest Cats, you also have to make physical accommodations for them. They can't be together all the time, or you'll have unplanned litters.

Do you live in a setting that is appropriate for a home business. Are you going to add on to your property? Will there be more traffic in and out? Are the neighbors or the homeowner's association going to create problems?

*What's your "Plan B?"*

Even the most optimistic ventures should include a plan for what happens if the endeavor fails. Can you keep the cats in your possession when you decide to halt your cattery operation? If not, do you have a plan for placing them?

The primary consideration is always the welfare of the animals. They are relying on you to protect them under all circumstances, including making sure they are well placed if you cannot keep them for any reason.

**Drawing Up Estimated Costs**

It's impossible to determine all the factors that affect set up costs. They are completely unique by individual circumstance.

You should, however, try to imagine every single thing you will need to purchase or alter, and get the best estimates you possibly can well in advance.

Your list of potential expenses should include:

*All necessary reference materials*

You may know a great deal about Norwegian Forest Cats, but now you will have to become conversant in the genetics of the breed.

*The cost of your foundation queen and/or stud*

If you can't afford to buy a breeding pair, you will also need to figure in the fees for pairing your animals with breeding stock from another cattery.

*Repeat veterinary tests*

Any time one of your animals goes "visiting" at another cattery, you will have to have FIV/FELV tests performed and produce proof of this fact.

*Routine and emergency veterinary expenses*

Remember, you're not only going to be paying for all the normal health checks and procedures, but also maternal and infant healthcare. Go over all the contingencies with your vet for worst case scenarios, like the need to perform C-Sections and include those items in your estimates.

*Cat equipment, furniture, and toys*

Multiply everything! More climbing trees, more beds, more travel crates, playpens for the kittens. It's possible you will create a whole cat "play room." Whatever figure you come up with, know that in this area, you always wind up spending more!

*Construction costs*

Yes, construction. It's extremely common for people who run catteries out of their homes to modify the structure in some way to facilitate their business or even to add on whole rooms. This is especially true if you are keeping intact animals of both genders that must be kept separated.

Don't fail to factor in an operating emergency reserve of at least 3-6 months. This will be crucial if you do decide to shut down your operation because it will give you time to get your animals placed.

## Showing Norwegian Forest Cats

Norwegian Forest Cat breeders show their animals not only to exhibit the excellence of their bloodlines, but also because the awards they garner lend prestige to their catteries. Breeders tend to be hardcore enthusiasts, and showing is an integral part of what they do.

Certainly someone who simply owns a beautiful Norwegian Forest Cat can participate in a cat show, although I am not a huge fan of these venues. Even the most well-socialized and gregarious cat is not all that thrilled with the show environment.

This is a purely personal decision for you, however, and I strongly recommend that your guiding principle be the personality of your cat. Especially if your cat is nervous around strangers (which Weegies typically are not) or if the animal dislikes noises and fast movements, a cat show is not going to be fun for Fluffy!

Attend some shows. Watch, learn, and then decide if the events are right for you and your cat. There are, however, some definite "rules" about what you do and do not do at a cat show.

## Chapter 5 – Breeding and Showing

**Attending a Cat Show**

If you hear nothing else about the etiquette of attending a cat show, hear this:

DON'T TOUCH!

Yes, the temptation is almost impossible to resist. You're surrounded by absolutely gorgeous and adorable cats of the highest quality. You want to pet every one. Don't even think about giving in to that urge!

The rule isn't to frustrate you, it's to protect the cats. Feline diseases are incredibly contagious and can be easily transmitted with just the touch of a nose. That same bacteria and those same viruses can and do live on your hands.

If an exhibitor at a cat show grants you permission to touch a cat, you are being afforded a high compliment. The invitation will be offered with an outstretched hand holding a bottle of sanitizer. Use it without blinking an eye.

The next cardinal rule? DON'T HELP.

If you hear someone yell, "LOOSE CAT," freeze. The only appropriate response is to stand still and be quiet. If you see the animal, signal the location to the owner, but under no circumstances should you attempt to be part of the retrieval.

Next on the list, MOVE.

Cat shows are hectic and busy. When an exhibitor is called to the ring, they have only a limited amount of time to get there or be disqualified. When someone yells, "Right of way," yield!

Don't be offended if you're talking to an exhibitor and that person suddenly stops talking, listens to the loudspeaker, and bolts for the ring without so much as a word. They trust you to know what's going on and not to be offended.

And finally, LISTEN.

When you are near the show ring and the judge begins to speak, be absolutely silent and listen. You do not want to distract the exhibitors or the cats. Also, the judge's comments on the breed will be highly educational. You'll learn a lot just by paying attention.

## How Cat Shows Operate

If you've ever attended a dog show, or watched one on TV, you are in no way prepared for what goes on at a cat show. There are a number of major differences.

Show cats are kept secured at all times and are only removed from their cages for judging. The overall atmosphere, however, is festive. Exhibitors go to great lengths to decorate their cages and the surrounding area.

Although the atmosphere is hectic, the pace can be glacial. There's a lot of time sitting around in between mad dashes to the ring.

Another key difference from dog shows is the class specifically designated for showing household pets. This attracts many young people to the competition, and is the place where some people start their active interest in the organized cat fancy.

The animals are evaluated by set breed standards formalized by the body officially sponsoring the show. The more an animal onforms to the points set out in the standard, the higher its score and performance in the show.

The major governing bodies of the cat fancy are listed below. Each has slightly different rules and show standards.) See the homepage of each organization for detailed explanations.)

- The International Cat Association
- Fédération Internationale Féline
- World Cat Federation
- Cat Fanciers Association
- Feline Federation Europe
- Australia Cat Federation
- American Association of Cat Enthusiasts
- American Cat Fanciers Association

## Final Thoughts on Breeding and Showing

Before you make any decisions regarding showing or breeding, learn everything you possibly can about Norwegian Forest Cats, and about catteries and cat shows.

You may love the idea of cultivating a beautiful line of cats, but loathe the notion of going anywhere near a show — or the show ring may look like fun and breeding like a nightmare.

You can do either, both, or neither! For most people simply have a beautiful Norwegian Forest Cat in their lives as a companion and friend is all the "award" they could ever possibly hope for. There is nothing that says owning a pedigreed cat means becoming deeply immersed in the world of the cat fancy.

At their best, breeding and showing are hobbies that should have only one goal in mind — the welfare of the cats. Living with and loving a cat, or any companion animal, however, is a commitment to a living creature that doesn't care about genetic quality or blue ribbon awards.

The bottom line is this. Decide what is right for you and your Norwegian Forest Cat and do that.

# Chapter 6 – Norwegian Cat Breeders

## US

### Alabama

Tryllekatt
Greg and Lynn Watts
E-mail: gregw@tryllekatt.com
Website: www.tryllekatt.com

### California

Sangha Cattery-Hermosa Beach
Melissa Morton
631-764-6288
E-Mail: Chasingstar999@aol.com
Website: www.sanghaforestcats.com

### Florida
Spree
Celeste Morvay
E-Mail: spreecattery@gmail.com
Website: www.spreecattery.com/

### Georgia
Nissekatt Cattery
Cumming
Sue and Jeff Shaw
770-844-1645
E-Mail: sueshaw@bellsouth.net

## Illinois

Norsestar Cattery
Frankfort
Margie & Scott Nelson
815-4693410
E-Mail: MarjNelson@aol.com
www.norsestarnfc.com/

## Iowa

Vanir Cats Cattery
Clive
Cheryl McConnell
515-987-1127
E-Mail: VanirCats@aol.com
www.VanirCats.com

## Michigan

Mycoon Cattery
Romulus
Sheila Gira-Windom
734-941-0325
E-Mail: Wegies1st@comcast.net
www.homestead.com/CATTERY/Mycooncattery.html

**New Jersey**

Kashi Saga Cattery
Southern New Jersey - Philadelphia Area
Barbara Chronakis
E-Mail: pirate@comcast.net
Website: www.kashisaga.com

Purricats
James and Heidi Ennis
Email: purricats@gmail.com
Website: www.purricats.com

**North Carolina**

Wegiekatt Cattery
Charlotte
Patti Harriman
Email: patti@wegiekatt.com
Website: www.wegiekatt.com

**Ohio**

NordicTale
Cincinnati
Brook Cole
E-Mail: nordictale@msn.com
Website: www.nordictale.com

## Oklahoma

OklahomaCats
Edmond
Susan James
E-Mail: sjames@oklahomacats.com
Website: www.oklahomacats.com

## Pennsylvania

Marsh Creek Cattery
Downingtown
Elizabeth Dickinson
610-458-7107
E-Mail: liz@marshcreekcats.com

Norja Cattery
Jane Hayward
E-Mail: norjacats@aol.com

## Texas

Ouijakatz Cattery
Barbara Midura
E-Mail: inspectdim@aol.com
Website: www.ouijakatz.com

Kattpenn Cattery
Southlake
Kathryn Pennington
817-488-6633
E-Mail: katpenn.info@verizon.net
Website: www.katpenn.com

KSNORSKATT
Sharon Poer
E-Mail: spoer@consolidated.net
Website: www.ksnorskatt.com

Bywater
Wendy Barrington
E-Mail: wbarrington@gmail.com

# Afterword

Now that you've had a chance to learn more about the Norwegian Forest Cat, I hope you're as intrigued by these big, lovable beauties as I am. One great advantage of this semi-longhaired breed is its minimal grooming profile.

Certainly you'll be covered in cat hair in the spring when your Weegie sheds its dense winter coat for lighter summer wear, but that only lasts a couple of weeks. It's a real pleasure to be able to enjoy a cat with a flowing coat that only requires weekly brushing.

I especially like the Weegie's full ruff and well-furnished ears. The resulting look of the even, triangular head and mildly oblique eyes offers just a hint of this breed's wild origins.

With big males reaching 16 pounds / 7.3 kg, the Norwegian Forest Cat is a muscular athlete with incredible skills for climbing. Don't even think about having a Weegie without a first-rate cat tree.

These cats do well with families or singles. They are attentive and involved without being needy, although no breed should be left alone for extended periods of time.

A Norwegian Forest Cat may not yowl at the top of its lungs like a lonely Siamese, but the cat will certainly miss you. Quietly conversational and equipped with a powerful purring motor, your Weegie will be constant presence in whatever is going on in the house.

Highly adaptable and amenable to children, other pets, and even visitors, the Norwegian Forest Cat is one of the most popular large cat breeds for these well-proven qualities as well as its great physical beauty.

# Appendix I - TICA Norwegian Forest Cat Show Standard

*HEAD - 40 points*
Shape - 8
Ears - 8
Eyes - 8
Chin - 4
Muzzle - 4
Profile - 8

*BODY - 35 points*
Torso - 7
Legs - 7
Tail - 7
Boning - 7
Musculature - 7

*COAT AND COLOR - 25 points*
Length - 5
Texture - 20

*CATEGORY:* Traditional.

*DIVISION:* All.

*COLORS:* All.

*PERMISSIBLE OUTCROSSES:* None.

## HEAD:

*Shape:* Triangular, where all sides are equally long when measured from the outer base of the ears to the chin and between the outer base of the ears; good height when seen in profile; forehead is sloped back.

*Eyes:* Large, almond shaped, set obliquely. Alert expression. All eye
colors except odd-eyes or blue permitted regardless of coat color.  Odd-eyes and blue eyes permitted in white and with white only.

*Ears:* Large, wide at the base, arched forward as if listening, slightly rounded tips that appear pointed when lynx tips are present. Lynx tips and furnishings that extend beyond the outer edge of each ear are desirable.  The outer edge of the ear should follow the line of the head down to the chin.

*Muzzle:* Following the line of the triangular head, with no evidence of
pinch or snippiness.

*Profile:* Long, straight profile from tip of nose to brow without break in
line, i.e., no stop.

*Neck:* Muscular; medium in length.

*BODY:*

*Torso:* Medium long and substantial.

*Legs:* In proportion to the body length, with hind legs higher than fore
legs.

*Feet:* Large, round, well-tufted.

*Tail:* Long and bushy. Should be at least as long as the body.

*Boning:* Substantial.

*Musculature:* Strongly built and sturdy.

*COAT/COLOR:*

*Length:* Semi-long.

*Texture:* The dense, woolly undercoat is covered by a smooth, water repellant upper coat which consists of long, coarse and glossy hair covering the back and the sides. A fully coated cat has a full ruff and
britches.

*Colors:* All colors of all divisions of the traditional category are recognized including all colors with white. Any amount of white is allowed anywhere on the cat.

*OTHER:*

*Balance:* Muscular and well-proportioned.

*Condition:* Not applicable / assumed.

*Temperament:* Intelligent and independent.

## GENERAL DESCRIPTION:

The Norwegian Forest has evolved through the centuries as a product of its environment. They had to feed, defend, and protect themselves from the elements in the forests. Only the cats that were good hunters and fast to escape from predators survived.

Norwegian Forest cats that survived their first winter had the correct, semi-long water-repellant coat and were well-proportioned, strong and intelligent. These no nonsense traits carry into the show ring. The Norwegian Forest is intelligent, independent and alert to its surroundings.

A Norwegian Forest is large to medium-large size overall and strongly built. They are high on their legs, with a medium long, rectangular body. Their hind legs are higher than their fore legs. They are muscular and heavily boned.

Their head is triangular, with all three sides equal when measured between the outer base of each ear and from these points to the chin. The profile is long and straight with no break or stop and displays a strong chin.

Their eyes are expressive, large, wide almond-shaped, and set on an oblique tilt. Their ears are large, open and set in line with the triangular shape of the head. They may be well-tufted and have lynx tips. Their tail is long, flowing and carried high.

The Norwegian Forest is known for its dense, rich fur with a woolly undercoat covered by long, coarse guard hairs. This coat is warm and water-repellant. A fully coated cat has a full ruff and britches. In the summer, the coat is short. The coat feels dense, especially on tabbies.

Solid, bicolor and tricolor cats often have a softer coat. The length of the Norwegian Forest coat is semi-long, which means that it should not be as long as a Persian coat.

The overall appearance is of an alert, healthy, firm, muscular and well-proportioned cat. The males are large and imposing, often weighing 12-15 pounds or more. The females can be considerably smaller. This breed is not fully developed until 5 years of age.

## ALLOWANCES:

Buttons, spots and lockets allowed in all colors. Length of coat and density of undercoat vary with the seasons. Under no circumstances should a cat be penalized for having a semi-long coat. Coat is evaluated primarily on texture and quality. Allow for size difference between males and females. Very slow maturing of this breed should be taken into account. Mature males may have broader heads than females.

## PENALIZE:

Too small and finely built cats. Round or square head; profile with a break (stop). Round eyes. Ears too small or narrow at the base. Legs that are short, thin - not in proportion to the body, or cowhocked. Short tail. Cobby or extremely long body. Dry or silky texture on coat.

Temperament must be unchallenging; any sign of definite challenge shall disqualify. The cat may exhibit fear, seek to flee, or generally complain aloud but may not threaten to harm. In accordance with Show Rules, ARTICLE SIXTEEN, the following shall be considered mandatory disqualifications: a cat that bites (216.9), a cat showing evidence of intent to deceive (216.10), adult whole male cats not having two descended testicles (216.11), cats with all or part of the tail missing , except as authorized by a board approved standard (216.12.1), cats with more than five toes on each front foot and four toes on each back foot, unless proved the result of an injury or as authorized by a Board approved standard (216.12.2), visible or invisible tail faults if Board approved standard requires disqualification (216.12.4), crossed eyes if Board approved standard requires disqualification (216.12.5), total blindness (216.12.6), markedly smaller size, not in keeping with the breed (216.12.9), and depression of the sternum or unusually small diameter of the rib cage itself (216.12.11.1). See Show Rules, ARTICLE SIXTEEN for more comprehensive rules governing penalties and disqualifications

(*Source:* http://www.tica.org/members/publications/standards/nf.pdf )

# Appendix 2 - Plants That Are Toxic to Cats

*Source:* The Cat Fancier's Association at www.cfa.org, http://www.cfa.org/CatCare/HouseholdHazards/ToxicPlants.aspx (Accessed May 2013).

Of the plants on this list, lilies are especially dangerous to cats. If you have any of these plants, they should be kept completely away from the cat, or the cat should not be allowed into the area of the garden or yard where they are growing.

If your cat does eat any part of a poisonous plant, seek veterinary help for your pet immediately.

Almond (pits)

Aloe Vera

Alocasia

Amaryllis

Apple (seeds)

Apple Leaf Croton

Apricot (pits)

Arrowgrass

Asparagus Fern

Autumn Crocus

Avocado (fruit and pit)

Azalea Baby's Breath

Baneberry

Bayonet

Beargrass

Beech

Belladonna

Bird of Paradise

Bittersweet

Black-eyed Susan

Black Locust

Bleeding Heart

Bloodroot

Bluebonnet

Box

Boxwood

Branching Ivy

Buckeyes

Buddhist Pine

Burning Bush

Buttercup Cactus

Candelabra
Caladium
Calla Lily
Castor Bean
Ceriman
Charming Dieffenbachia
Cherry (pits, seeds, leaves)
Cherry Laurel
Chinaberry
Chinese Everegreen
Christmas Rose
Chrysanthemum
Cineria
Clematis
Cordatum
Coriaria
Cornflower
Corn Plant
Cornstalk Plant
Croton
Corydalis
Crocus, Autumn
Crown of Thorns
Cuban Laurel
Cutleaf Philodendron
Cycads
Cyclamen
Daffodil
Daphne
Datura
Deadly Nightshade

Death Camas
Devil's Ivy
Delphinium
Decentrea
Dieffenbachia
Dracaena Palm
Dragon Tree
Dumb Cane
Easter Lily
Eggplant
Elaine
Elderberry
Elephant Ear
Emerald Feather
English Ivy
Eucalyptus
Euonymus
Evergreen Ferns
Fiddle-leaf Fig
Florida Beauty
Flax
Four O'Clock
Foxglove
Fruit Salad Plant
Geranium
German Ivy
Giant Dumb Cane
Glacier Ivy
Golden Chain
Gold Dieffenbachia
Gold Dust Dracaena

Golden Glow
Golden Pothos
Gopher Purge
Hahn's Self-Branching Ivy
Heartland Philodendron
Hellebore
Hemlock, Poison
Hemlock, Water
Henbane
Holly
Horsebeans
Horsebrush
Hellebore
Horse Chestnuts
Hurricane Plant
Hyacinth
Hydrangea
Indian Rubber Plant
Indian Tobacco
Iris
Iris Ivy
Jack in the Pulpit
Janet Craig Dracaena
Japanese Show Lily
Java Beans
Jessamine
Jerusalem Cherry
Jimson Weed
Jonquil
Jungle Trumpets
Kalanchoe

Lacy Tree Philodendron
Lantana
Larkspur
Laurel
Lily
Lily Spider
Lily of the Valley
Locoweed
Lupine
Madagascar Dragon Tree
Marble Queen
Marigold
Marijuana
Mescal Bean
Mexican Breadfruit
Miniature Croton
Mistletoe
Mock Orange
Monkshood
Moonseed
Morning Glory
Mother-in-Law's Tongue
Morning Glory
Mountain Laurel
Mushrooms
Narcissus
Needlepoint Ivy
Nephytis
Nightshade Oleander
Onion
Oriental Lily

# Appendix 2 - Plants That Are Toxic to Cats

Peace Lily
Peach (pits and leaves)
Pencil Cactus
Peony
Periwinkle
Philodendron
Pimpernel
Plumosa Fern
Poinciana
Poinsettia (low toxicity)
Poison Hemlock
Poison Ivy
Poison Oak
Pokeweed
Poppy
Potato
Pothos
Precatory Bean
Primrose
Privet, Common
Red Emerald
Red Princess
Red-Margined Dracaena
Rhododendron
Rhubarb
Ribbon Plan
Rosemary Pea
Rubber Plant
Saddle Leaf Philodendron
Sago Palm
Satin Pathos

Schefflera
Scotch Broom
Silver Pothos
Skunk Cabbage
Snowdrops
Snow on the Mountain
Spotted Dumb Cane
Staggerweed
Star of Bethlehem
String of Pearls
Striped Dracaena
Sweetheart Ivy
Sweetpea
Swiss Cheese plant
Tansy Mustard
Taro Vine
Tiger Lily
Tobacco
Tomato Plant (green fruit, stem, leaves)
Tree Philodendron
Tropic Snow Dieffenbachia
Tulip
Tung Tree
Virginia Creeper
Water Hemlock
Weeping Fig
Wild Call
Wisteria Yews
English Yew
Western Yew
American Yew

# Relevant Websites

**Vetstreet: Norwegian Forest Cats**
www.vetstreet.com/cats/norwegian-forest-cat

**Cat Fancier's Association Breed Profile**
www.cfainc.org/Breeds/BreedsKthruR/NorwegianForestCa
t.aspx

**Norwegian Cat Fancier's Association**
www.cfainc.org/Breeds/BreedsKthruR/NorwegianForestCa
t.aspx

**Glycogen Storage Disease in Norwegian Forest Cats**
www.forestcats.net/articles/article_gsd_iv.html

**Feline Hip Dysplasia**
www.forestcats.net/articles/article_feline_hip_dysplasia.ht
ml

**Feline Hypertrophic Cardiomyopathy: Advice for
Breeders**
www.forestcats.net/articles/article_feline_hypertrophic_car
diomyopathy

**Norwegian Forest Cat HCM Research**
www.nfchcm.com

**Norwegian Forest Cat Breed Council**
www.nfcbc.org

**Norwegian Forest Cat Forum (Europe)**
www.forum.norwegianforestcat.eu/

**Norwegian Forest Cat Breed Club (US)**
www.norwegianforestcatbreedclub.org

**The Norwegian Forest Cat Club (UK)**
www.nfcc.co.uk

**The Norwegian Forest Cat Society (UK)**
www.tnfcs.co.uk/

**Norwegian Forest Cat Rescue Groups**
norwegianforestcat.rescueshelter.com

**Norwegian Forest Cat Breeders in Australia**
www.cat-world.com.au/norwegian-forest-cat-breeders-in-australia

**New Zealand Cat Fancy: Norwegian Forest Cat**
www.nzcatfancy.gen.nz

# Frequently Asked Questions

Although it's recommended that you read the entire text to really understand Norwegian Forest Cats and their care needs, these are some of the frequently asked questions about "Weegies."

**Are Norwegian Forest Cats big?**

They certainly can be. Some big males reach 16 lbs./7.3 kg, but small females may weigh just 10 lbs./4.5 kg. They are roughly the same size as Maine Coons, and certainly look bigger than they are thanks to their lush semi-longhaired coats.

**Are Norwegian Forest Cats a natural breed?**

Yes, Norwegian Forest Cats are believed to be descended from wild cats in Norway. Their ancestors most likely traveled on Viking ships to provide rodent control.

The breed is thought to have been crossed with longhaired cats brought back to Europe by the crusaders. Norwegian Forest Cats nearly went extinct as a distinct breed before World War II, but were saved by dedicated enthusiasts that developed a breeding program to save the line.

**Do Norwegian Forest Cats require a lot of grooming?**

Surprisingly, Norwegian Forest Cats are quite easy to groom, needing no more than a once-a-week brushing, with more help required during their annual spring shedding season.

**Is there any difference in disposition between male and females?**

There really is no difference in disposition with male and female Norwegian Forest Cats. When you adopt your cat from a breeder, you will be required to have the kitten either spayed or neutered, which further negates any perceived differences.

Some people worry about male cats spraying urine in the house, but this behavior is rarely if ever seen in neutered males. Both genders have equally pleasant, adaptable, and easy-going personalities.

**Should I get one kitten or two?**

Since cats are not the aloof loners they are popularly believed to be, any cat will benefit from having a "friend" of its own kind.

If you have never adopted two cats from the same litter, you may not know the special bond that siblings maintain throughout their lives. This can be a joy both for you and your cats.

The real determination should always be if you have room and time for two cats, because whether your Norwegian Forest Cat has a feline buddy or not, your pet or pets will bond strongly with you and want your attention and interaction.

**Is the Norwegian Forest Cat's coat waterproof?**

It is really more accurate to say that the double coat is water resistant. It take a lot for moisture to penetrate the top layer of fur and reach the skin, which is an adaptation that served these cats well during the winter in their Scandinavian land of origin.

**Are Norwegian Forest Cats any more or less prone to effect people with allergies?**

This is certainly not a hypoallergenic breed, and Norwegian Forest Cats do shed. If you are allergic to cats, you will likely have an adverse reaction to this breed. (The reaction is actually to the protein Fel d 1.)

**What's the difference between the Maine Coon and Norwegian Forest Cats?**

Maine Coons are much more rectangular cats while Weegies stand taller in the hindquarters. Also, the Norwegian Forest Cat has a triangular head, while the Maine Coon is square at the muzzle.

The Norwegian Forest Cat's outer coat is rather stiff and somewhat coarse, but Maine Coons are silky and soft. In disposition, however, the two breeds are quite similar.

**Do Norwegian Forest Cats get along with dogs?**

Yes, they do, quite well indeed. The Norwegian Forest Cat is often referred to as a "dog lover's cat." Frequently a Weegie will get along much better with a dog than with a new cat introduced into the house.

**Do Norwegian Forest Cats need anything special to be happy?**

Yes, with this breed you absolutely must have a really good, interesting cat "tree." Weegies love to climb and they're so good at it they'll even go up rocks! Invest in the biggest, most extensive, and interesting cat tree you can find.

**How much do Norwegian Forest Cats cost?**

Pet quality Norwegian Forest Cats typically cost between $885 (£550) and $1375 (£853). If you are interested in a show quality animal, the price could easily double and more.

**How long do Norwegian Forest Cats live?**

A well cared for Norwegian Forest Cat kept exclusively indoors (which is recommended) should live 14-16 years if provided with routine veterinary care and high quality nutrition.

**Are there any specific health conditions associated with this breed?**

Yes, Norwegian Forest cats are prone to developing hypertrophic cardiomyopathy, hip dysplasia, and glycogen storage disease. See Chapter 3 on health for more information.

**Why should I buy from a breeder?**

Well, for one thing, buying from an established breeder is the only way to make sure you are indeed buying a Norwegian Forest cat. Also, breeders routinely have their cats screened for known genetic issues.

Obtaining your pet from a good cattery will give you the confidence that you are adopting a healthy kitten, and you will be able to turn to the breeder for any advice or information you need in the future.

**Can I make money breeding cats?**

The only reason anyone should ever become a cat breeder is love of the breed. Running a cattery, no matter how much you charge for your kittens, is a labor of love. Most cat breeders will tell you that in a good year, they just do break even.

Do not even think of raising this breed or any animal for that matter for the exclusive purpose of making money. If you don't love the animals, don't breed and raise them.

**Can I show my cat?**

It is certainly possible for an enthusiast in possession of an exceptionally fine Norwegian Forest Cat to show the animal, but you should understand that most catteries sell only "pet quality" kittens for prices the general public can afford. If you really want a show quality Weegie, the purchase price could easily double and then some.

# Glossary

## A

Ailurophile - A person who loves cats.

Ailurophobe - A person who fears or even hates cat.

Allergen - In relation to cats, the primary allergen, the substance that causes an allergic reaction in some people, is, Fel d 1, a protein produced by the cat's sebaceous glands, and present in its saliva.

Allergy - A high level of sensitivity present in some people to a given substance, like the protein Fel d 1 in cats. Generally the reaction includes, but is not limited to watering eyes, sneezing, itching, and skin rashes.

Alter - A term which refers to the neutering or spaying of a cat or dog.

## B

Bloodline - The verifiable line of descent that establishes an animal's pedigree.

Breed Standard - A set of standards for a given breed formulated by parent breed clubs and used as the basis for evaluating show quality animals.

# Glossary

**Breed** - Term that refers to a group of cats with defined physical characteristics that are related by common ancestry.

**Breeder** - A person who works with a particular breed of cats, producing offspring from high-quality dams and sires for the purpose of maintaining and improving the genetic quality of the line.

**Breeding** - The process in which dams and sires are paired for the purpose of producing offspring.

**Breeding Program** - An organized and ongoing program in which cats are mated selectively to produce offspring that are ideal examples of the breed.

**Breeding Quality** - A term describing a cat that meets the standards of a given breed to a degree sufficient to be included in a breeding program.

**Breed True** - The phrase which describes the capacity of a male and female cat to produce kittens that closely resemble themselves in accepted elements of the breed standard.

## C

**Carpal Pads** - Located on a cat's front legs at the "wrists," these pads provide added traction for the animal's gait.

# Glossary

Castrate - The medical procedure whereby a male cat's testicles are removed.

Caterwaul - A feline vocalization that produces a discordant, shrill sound.

Cat Fancy - Term used to describe the overall group of registered associations clubs, and individuals that breed and show cats.

Catnip - A member of the mint family, this aromatic perennial herb (Nepeta cataria) contains an oil to which some cats are strongly attracted and to which they respond with a kind of "stoned" intoxication. Kittens cannot respond to catnip until they are 8-9 months of age.

Cattery - Any establishment that exists for the purpose of housing cats, and where they are bred as part of an organized program.

Certified Pedigree - A pedigree that has been issued in an official capacity by a feline registering association.

Clowder - A collective term for a group of cats.

Coat - Term referring to a cat's fur.

Crate - Container used to safely transport cats from one location to another or to confine them temporarily for their own safety.

Glossary

Crepuscular - Although known in popular lore as nocturnal animals, cats are actually crepuscular, meaning they are most active at dusk and dawn.

Crossbred - A cat that is the product of breeding a sire and a dam of different breeds.

# D

Dam -The female in a parenting set of cats.

Dander - The small scale of hair and skin that are shed by an animal. Often responsible for allergic reactions in individuals with a sensitivity to the substance.

Declawing - A highly controversial surgical procedure that removes a cat's claws permanently.

Desex - Describes the alteration of an animal by neutering or spaying.

Domesticated - Animals that have been tamed to live with or work with humans, or that have chosen to cultivate such a relationship.

# E

Ear Mites - Microscopic parasites that feed on the lining of a cat's ear canal, causing debris to build up, generating a foul odor, and resulting in extreme itching.

# Glossary

Entire - A term describing a cat that has an intact reproductive system.

Exhibitor - An individual that participates in organized cat shows.

## F

Fel d 1 - A protein produced by the cat's sebaceous glands, and present in its saliva, which causes an allergic reaction in some people.

Feline - A member of the family Felidae. Includes lions, tigers, jaguars, and wild and domestic cats.

Fleas - Various bloodsucking insects of the order Siphonaptera. They are wingless, and their legs are adapted for jumping. They are parasitical, and feed off warm-blooded animals.

Flehmening/Flehmen Reaction - A facial gesture in cats that is often mistaken for a grimace. In reality, the cat is drawing in air to pass it over a special structure in the roof of the mouth called the Jacobsen's Organ, which functions as a second set of nostrils and allows cats to "taste" a scent.

## G

Gene pool - In a population of organisms, the "gene pool" is the collective genetic information relative to reproduction.

# Glossary

**Genes** - Determine particular characteristics in a given organism. They are a distinct hereditary unit and consist of a DNA sequence occupying a specific location on a chromosome.

**Genetic** - Refers to any trait, characteristic, tendency, or condition that is inherited.

**Genetically Linked Defects** - Health specific problems or those relative to temperament that are passed from one generation to the next.

**Genetics** - The scientific study of heredity.

**Genotype** - Refers to the genetic makeup of an organism or a group of organisms.

**Groom** - The act of caring for the coat of a feline, which may include brushing, combing, trimming, or washing.

**Guard Hair** - Long, coarse hairs that form the outer layer of a cat's coat.

**H**

**Heat** - The seasonal estrus cycle of a female cat (or any other mammal).

**Hereditary** - Any characteristic, trait, disease, or condition that can be genetically transmitted from parent to offspring.

# Glossary

Histamine - A physiologically active amine in plant and animal tissue released from mast cells as part of an allergic reaction in humans.

Hock - Anatomical term describing the ankle of a cat's hind leg.

Household Pet - A cat not registered to be exhibited or shown in competition.

Housetraining - The process whereby a cat is trained to use a litter box to live cleanly in a house.

Humane Societies - Any one of a number of groups that work to put an end to animal suffering due to overt acts of cruelty and other impoverishing or harmful circumstances.

# I

Immunization - The use of inoculations to create immunity against disease. Also referred to as vaccination.

Innate - A quality, trait, or tendency present at birth and thus inborn

Inbreeding - When two closely-related cats of the same breed are mated.

Instinct - A pattern of behavior in a species that is inborn and comes in response to specific environmental stimuli.

Intact - Animals that are intact possess their complete reproductive system. They have not been neutered or spayed.

# J

Jacobsen's Organ - An organ located in the roof of a cat's mouth that allows it to "taste" a scent. Appears as two small openings and is regarded as a second set of "nostrils."

# K

Kindle - A collective term for a group of kittens. An alternate term is "chowder."

Kitten - Young cats under the age of 6 months.

# L

Lactation - Process by which the mammary glands form and secrete milk.

Lactating - Term used for a mammalian mother when she is secreting or producing milk.

Litter - The number of offspring in a single birth. Generally 3-4 in cats, although 6-10 is not uncommon.

Litter Box - A container filled with commercial kitty litter or sand and used in the home as a sanitary and manageable location for a cat to urinate and defecate.

# Glossary

Longhair - Cats with varying lengths of long hair, typically with plumed tails and prominent neck ruffs.

## M

Mites - Small arachnids (of the order Acarina) that are parasites on animals and plants. Often seen in the ears of felines.

Moggy - The term for a mixed breed cat in the United Kingdom.

Muzzle - In cats, the part of the head projecting forward including the mouth, nose, and jaws. May also be referred to as the snout.

## N

Neuter - The term used to describe castrating a male cat.

Nictitating Membrane - A cat's third eyelid, which is a transparent inner eyelid that serves to protect and moisten the eye.

Nocturnal - Term used to describe animals that are most active at night. It is mistakenly applied to cats, who are actually crepuscular, being most active at dawn and dusk.

## O

Odd-Eyed - Eyes of two different colors presenting in a single individual.

## P

Papers - The documentation of a cat's pedigree and registration.

Pedigree - A cat's genealogy presented in writing and spanning three or more generations.

Pet Quality - A cat that does not sufficiently meet the accepted standard for its breed to be shown in competition or to be used in a breeding program.

## Q

Queen - An intact female cat, one that has not been spayed.

Quick - The vascular portion of a cat's claw that will, if clipped, bleed profusely.

## R

Rabies - A viral disease that is highly infections and typically fatal to warm blooded animals. It attacks the central nervous system and is transmitted by the bite of an infected animal.

# Glossary

Recognition - The point at which a cat breed is officially accepted under a cat fancy organization's rules.

Registered Cat - A cat registered through a recognized feline association that has documentation of its ancestry.

Registered Name - The official name used by a registered cat, which is typically long and reflective of its ancestry.

Registration - The record of the particulars of a cat's birth and ancestry filed with an official organization.

Scratching Post - A tower-like structure covered in carpet or rope that allows a cat to sharpen and clean its claws inside the house without being destructive to furniture.

## S

Secondary Coat - In a cat, the fine hairs of the undercoat.

Semi-Longhair - Long-haired cats with a medium-length coat.

Shelter - Any local organization that exists for the purpose of rescuing and caring for homeless and stray animals. Also works to find permanent homes for these animals.

Show - An organized exhibition in which judges evaluate cats according to accepted standard for each breed and make awards accordingly.

Show Cat - Cats that participate in shows.

Show Quality - Cats that meet the standards for their breed at a sufficient level to compete in organized cat shows.

Show Standard - A description of the ideal qualities of a breed of cats used as the basis for which the cats are judged in competition. Also known as standard of point.

Sire - The male member of a parenting set of cats.

Spay - The surgery to remove a female cat's ovaries.

Spray - A territorial behavior typically seen in male cats whereby the animal emits a stream of urine as a marker.

Stud - An intact male cat that has not been altered and is used as part of a breeding program.

Subcutaneous - Placed just below the skin, as in an injection.

**T**

Tapetum Lucidum - The interior portion of a cat's eye that aids in night vision and is highly reflective.

**U**

Undercoat - The layer of a cat's coat that is composed of down hairs.

# Glossary

Undercolor - The color of the hair lying closest to a cat's skin.

## V

Vaccine - A weakened or dead preparation of a bacterium, virus, or other pathogen used to stimulate the production of antibodies for the purpose of creating immunity against the disease when injected.

## W

Wean - The point at which a kitten begins to eat solid food and is taken off its mother's milk as the primary source of nutrition.

Whisker Break - Refers to an indentation of the upper jaw on a cat.

Whisker Pad - The thickened or fatty pads on either side of a cat's face holding rows of sensory whiskers.

Whole - A cat of either gender that is intact, and has not been neutered or spayed.

# Index

# Index

.html

16116516R00076

Printed in Poland
by Amazon Fulfillment
Poland Sp. z o.o., Wrocław